THE LITTLE BOOK OF SELF-REGULATION ACTIVITIES FOR KIDS

THE LITTLE BOOK OF SELF-REGULATION ACTIVITIES FOR KIDS

FOR AGES 8–11

50 CBT Exercises and **Coping Strategies** to Help Children Handle Anxiety, Stress, and Other Strong Emotions

Jenna Berman, LCSW

ULYSSES BOOKS
FOR YOUNG READERS

Published in 2026 by

an imprint of The Stable Book Group
32 Court Street, Suite 2109
Brooklyn, NY 11201
www.ulyssespress.com

ISBN: 978-1-64604-892-2
eISBN: 978-1-64604-893-9

Artwork from Shutterstock.com

Printed in the United States
10 9 8 7 6 5 4 3 2 1

IMPORTANT NOTE TO READERS: This book has been written and published for informational and educational purposes only. It is not intended to serve as medical advice or to be any form of medical treatment. You should always consult with your physician before altering or changing any aspect of your medical treatment. Do not stop or change any prescription medications without the guidance and advice of your physician. Any use of the information in this book is made on the reader's good judgment and is the reader's sole responsibility. This book is not intended to diagnose or treat any medical condition and is not a substitute for a physician.

To Natasha and Teddy,
who teach me every day.

INTRODUCTION

Games can be a powerful way to learn and practice tools that help you to identify, understand, and take control of feelings. These activities can be used on their own or attached to another game. A couple of ideas:

- ❑ **Play basketball or finger-flick football!** If you make a basket or score a goal, ask another player a question from *The Little Book of Self-Regulation Activities for Kids*. If you miss, pick a card and answer a question from *The Little Book of Self-Regulation Activities for Kids*.
- ❑ **Play a card game!** Place a standard deck face down and choose a card from the top of the pile. If you play an even or odd number, pick a card and answer a question from *The Little Book of Self-Regulation Activities for Kids*. If you play a face card, do something silly.

While the questions and directives within these pages will always be the same, it can be beneficial to use them time and time again. The more we think about and practice cognitive behavioral techniques, the more likely we will be able to access them when we are faced with difficult-to-navigate feelings, unhelpful thoughts, and unhelpful urges.

Have fun as you build skills that will empower you to experience big emotions and be in control!

ACTIVITY 1

Name one to five emotions that you are experiencing right now. Some possibilities include:

- ❑ Angry
- ❑ Bored
- ❑ Cautious
- ❑ Confident
- ❑ Confused
- ❑ Disgusted
- ❑ Ecstatic
- ❑ Embarrassed
- ❑ Enraged
- ❑ Exhausted
- ❑ Frightened
- ❑ Frustrated
- ❑ Guilty
- ❑ Happy
- ❑ Hopeful
- ❑ Jealous
- ❑ Lonely
- ❑ Mischievous
- ❑ Overwhelmed
- ❑ Proud
- ❑ Sad
- ❑ Shocked
- ❑ Shy
- ❑ Surprised
- ❑ Suspicious
- ❑ Worried

ACTIVITY 2

Talk about a time when you felt **disappointed** or about something that would make you feel disappointed.

ACTIVITY 3

When we have a feeling, it gives us the urge to do something. Sometimes our urges are helpful, and sometimes they are unhelpful. We can have an urge and make a different choice. **Talk about a time when you felt bored.** What urge did you have? Did you act on that urge? Was it helpful or unhelpful?

ACTIVITY 4

Sometimes our feelings can make us have thoughts that aren't true and aren't helpful. **Talk about a time when you felt uncomfortable.** What were you thinking? Were those thoughts helpful or unhelpful?

ACTIVITY 5

Talk about a time when you felt angry. Act out this moment, then freeze like a statue. Hold the statue pose for 30 seconds. Notice the feelings in your body and what your body is doing. When the 30 seconds have passed, describe what you noticed.

ACTIVITY 6

Talk about a time when you felt proud of yourself. Which of your positive qualities does this memory illustrate?

ACTIVITY 7

Sometimes feelings are big, and sometimes feelings are small. We can rate how strong our feelings are with a **Feelings Thermometer**. **Name events that trigger you to feel a 1, 5, and 10 of pride** on the Feelings Thermometer.

ACTIVITY 8

Sometimes feelings are big, and sometimes feelings are small. We can rate how strong our feelings are with a **Feelings Thermometer. Name events that trigger you to feel a 1, 5, and 10 of frustration** on the Feelings Thermometer.

ACTIVITY 9

Even on crummy days, we can experience joy. Noticing the little things that bring us joy can help to make the unpleasant things a little easier to tolerate. What is something that brought you joy today? **This can be something that brought you a lot of joy, such as playing a fun game, or just a little bit of joy, such as eating something tasty.**

ACTIVITY 10

When we have feelings, our bodies respond, often preparing us for a fight, flight, or freeze reaction. Imagine that you are walking in the jungle and a lion starts chasing you. **RUN!** Run in place as fast as you can for 30 seconds. While running, check the following:

- ❑ Are your muscles tight or relaxed?
- ❑ Is your breathing fast or slow?
- ❑ Is your breathing moving your belly or your chest?
- ❑ Is your heart beating fast or slow?

Note: Your muscles, breathing, and heart may react similarly when you experience unpleasant emotions such as fear.

ACTIVITY 11

Try this relaxation technique!

Belly Button Breathing: Find a comfortable position sitting in a chair. Put your finger in your belly button. Notice if your belly is rising and falling with each breath. If it's not, shift your breathing so that it does. Breathe in through your nose for about four seconds and breathe out through your mouth for about five to eight seconds. Do this for one minute.

ACTIVITY 12

Try this relaxation technique!

Toy Breathing: Find a comfortable position lying down. Place a stuffed animal or other small, light toy over your belly button. Watch the toy go up as you breathe in and down as you breathe out. If the toy is not rising and falling, shift your breathing so that it does. Continue breathing and watching the toy go up and down with each breath for one minute.

ACTIVITY 13

Try this relaxation technique!

One-Nostril Breathing: Hold one of your nostrils closed with your finger and close your mouth. Slowly breathe in and out through the other nostril. Do this for one minute.

ACTIVITY 14

Try this relaxation technique!

The Chair Technique: Sit in a chair with your feet flat on the ground. Grab underneath the chair with your hands and pull up with all of your strength. Press your feet into the ground and push down with all of your strength. Count to 10 as you continue to pull up with your arms and push down with your feet. When you get to 10, completely relax your muscles. Feel the difference between tense and relaxed. Try to wiggle out any tension that's left over in your body.

ACTIVITY 15

Try this relaxation technique!

Shake Out the Stress: Shake your hands as if you're trying to dry water off of them. Imagine all of your stress and tension flying out of your fingertips as you continue to shake them as fast as possible for 10 seconds. Drop your hands down by your sides. Your fingers might feel tingly. Take a few deep breaths and notice any relaxed or tingly sensations in your arms and hands.

ACTIVITY 16

Try this relaxation technique!

Roll Out the Stress: Slowly roll your shoulders forward three times, and then slowly roll your shoulders back three times. Press your shoulders down, making the space between your shoulders and ears as wide as possible. Slowly press your left ear down toward your left shoulder and then press your right ear down toward your right shoulder. Bring your head back to a neutral position.

ACTIVITY 17

Our feelings are shaped by the ways we think about the things happening. Imagine that you are excited to eat a bagel for breakfast but discover that your mom ate the last one. You think, "Why would she do that?! Now I have nothing to eat! She knew I was going to eat the bagel!" How would this thought make you feel? What's a different, more helpful way that you can think about the situation?

ACTIVITY 18

Our thoughts can shape the ways we want to react to the things happening around us. Imagine you have to get a shot and you think, "This is going to hurt too badly. I can't handle the pain that the shot is going to cause." What urge would you have, or what would you automatically want to do? Would acting on this urge be good for you? What's a different, more helpful and rational way that you can think about getting a shot?

ACTIVITY 19

All-or-Nothing thinking is an unhelpful thinking pattern when we see things in black-and-white categories. Things are either good or bad. It has to be one way or you see it as not okay. Give an example of an All-or-Nothing thought.

ACTIVITY 20

Overgeneralization is a common unhelpful thinking pattern when we see a single negative event as a never-ending pattern of defeat. We think this is always going to happen, or this will always be the way it is. Give an example of Overgeneralization.

ACTIVITY 21

Labeling is a common unhelpful thinking pattern when we label and mislabel things, describing them with words that are loaded with feelings. Instead of describing your mistake, you see yourself as something negative. When someone else does something that you don't like, you attach a negative label to that person. Give an example of a Labeling thought.

ACTIVITY 22

Mental Filtering is a common unhelpful thinking pattern when we pick out a negative detail and focus only on that. Like a drop of ink that changes the color of an entire cup of water, this type of thinking darkens the way we see things. Give an example of Mental Filtering.

ACTIVITY 23

Disqualifying the Positive is a common unhelpful thinking pattern when we think positive things don't count for one reason or another. Give an example of Disqualifying the Positive.

ACTIVITY 24

Mind Reading is a common unhelpful thinking pattern when we assume that someone is having negative thoughts about us. Give an example of Mind Reading.

ACTIVITY 25

The Fortune-Teller Error is a common unhelpful thinking pattern when we think that things will turn out badly and feel as if the bad thing is definitely going to happen. We might believe we can't deal with the bad thing if it happens, even if it would just be uncomfortable. Give an example of a Fortune-Teller Error.

ACTIVITY 26

Magnification or **Minimization** is a common unhelpful thinking pattern when we blow up the importance of things or shrink things until they seem tiny. Give an example of a Magnification or Minimization.

ACTIVITY 27

Emotional Reasoning is a common unhelpful thinking pattern when we believe something must be true just because we feel that way, even if there are no facts that support our belief. Give an example of an Emotional Reasoning thought.

ACTIVITY 28

"Should" and **"Must" Statements** show a common unhelpful thinking pattern when we think there is a certain way that everyone, including ourselves, should do things. We make it a big deal in our heads when things don't go the way we think they should. Give an example of a "Should" or "Must" Statement.

ACTIVITY 29

Personalization is a common unhelpful thinking pattern when we blame ourselves for something negative that happened or someone's negative behavior, even if it's possible or likely that there's another explanation. Give an example of Personalization.

ACTIVITY 30

Broken Record Player Thinking is a common unhelpful thinking pattern when we brood about something on repeat that may be true but is not helpful to focus on. Has there ever been a time in your life when you thought about something on repeat? What did doing this cause—for both your emotions and your actions?

ACTIVITY 31

Tunnel Vision is a common unhelpful thinking pattern when we only see the parts of a situation that are bad. Give an example of Tunnel Vision.

ACTIVITY 32

Imagine that you are about to ask a group of kids if you can sit with them at lunch. What is the worst thing that could happen? If that happened, how could you deal with it? What is the best thing that could happen?

ACTIVITY 33

Imagine you are doing math homework and there's a question that is super confusing for you. You ask your dad for help and he encourages you to think about it and keep trying. You think, "He's so mean! He should just tell me what to do! I can't do this!" **How can you talk back to this unhelpful thought?**

ACTIVITY 34

Imagine that you failed a test. For the rest of the day, you keep thinking on repeat, "I failed the test. I failed the test. I failed the test..." It is unhelpful to keep having this thought. **What is something that you can think about, do, and/or say to yourself to help you shift your thinking and shift your mood?**

ACTIVITY 35

Listening to music is a coping tool that can help us to take a break from unhelpful thoughts and shift our moods. Think of songs that make you feel happy or relaxed. **Name three of these songs that you could put on a feel-good playlist.**

ACTIVITY 36

A **Mental Vacation** can help us to take a break from focusing on stressful thoughts, feelings, and situations, and to chill out how strong our feelings are. **Think of a place where you've actually been that makes you feel calm and relaxed.** Describe this place in as many details as possible using all of your senses. Describe what you enjoy doing here. You can return here in your mind any time you choose.

ACTIVITY 37

When having unhelpful thoughts about the past or future, we can take control of our thinking and emotions by using all of our senses to bring our awareness to the moment. Try doing this now with the **5, 4, 3, 2, 1 Coping Tool**:

- ❑ **5:** Name 5 things you can see.
- ❑ **4:** Name 4 things you can touch. Actually touch them.
- ❑ **3:** Name 3 things you can hear (outside of your head–no thoughts).
- ❑ **2:** Name 2 things you can smell. Actually smell them.
- ❑ **1:** Notice what your mouth tastes like (bonus: taste something yummy if you can/ want).

ACTIVITY 38

All people have qualities that make them awesome. Sometimes our unhelpful thoughts make it hard to remember our strengths. **Ask someone to identify something they like about you.**

ACTIVITY 39

Harper invited friends over for a sleepover. Nobody was available. She later found out that they all went to a sleepover at another girl's house that night. Harper felt sad, lonely, embarrassed, and angry. She had the urge to avoid seeing them for as long as possible, but she knew that would not be good for her. How can Harper:

- ❑ Try to solve the problem?
- ❑ Make herself feel better about the problem?
- ❑ Let it go and move on?

If you were in Harper's situation, which one of these choices would you make?

Note: You can make more than one choice.

ACTIVITY 40

Matteo's parents have strict screen-time rules. He gets frustrated that he can't play and talk with his friends for as long as he wants to. Matteo has been sneaking online at night, but knows it isn't good for him. He's been tired because of how late he is up, and he is worried that his parents will catch him. How can Matteo:

❑ Try to solve the problem?

❑ Make himself feel better about the problem?

❑ Let it go and move on?

If you were in Matteo's situation, which of these choices would you make?

Note: You can make more than one choice.

ACTIVITY 41

Everything we do is a choice, and every choice we make causes something to happen. **Talk about a choice you made that felt good in the moment but caused something that made you feel worse later.** What is another choice you could have made in this situation?

ACTIVITY 42

We can choose our actions by thinking about what we want to cause. What is something you want to cause? This can be a big goal, such as getting good grades, or something smaller, such as cleaning your room. **What are three choices that you can make that will take you closer to this thing that you want to cause?**

ACTIVITY 43

We can choose our actions by thinking about who we want to be in the world. Imagine there is a movie about your life. How would you want to be described in the trailer for the movie? **What are three choices that you can make that would be described by the qualities portrayed?**

ACTIVITY 44

Imagine you are working on a group project in class. The other kids in your group are goofing off but you are following directions. The teacher yells at your group and says that this behavior is going to negatively affect your grade on the project.

STOP: Ask yourself, "What is happening? What am I thinking? How am I feeling about it?"

THINK: Identify three choices you can make in this situation. Note: This can include unhelpful choices that you might have the urge to make.

GO: What is each choice likely to cause? How would that make you feel? Pick the choice that would be best for you.

ACTIVITY 45

We can use the Choice Rating Scale below to help us make good choices. Imagine you are playing a game with your friend. Your friend won. You feel super frustrated and disappointed that you lost. You want to have fun with your friend and avoid a fight. What choice could you make for each rating on the **Choice Rating Scale**:

1	2	3
This choice will take me closer to the things I want to cause.	This choice will not take me closer to, or further away, from the things I want to cause.	This choice will take me further away from the things I want to cause.

ACTIVITY 46

Mistakes are opportunities to learn and grow. **Talk about a mistake you made.** What did you learn from this mistake? How can you try to use this lesson to help you do things differently in the future?

ACTIVITY 47

What is something that would trigger you to feel worried? What could you say to yourself and/or do that would help you to feel a little less worried in this situation?

ACTIVITY 48

Talk about a time when your feelings were in control and you reacted in a way that was not good for you. How could you have:

1. Tried to solve the problem?

2. Made yourself feel better about the problem?

3. Let it go and moved on?

If you could go back in time, what choice(s) would you make?

ACTIVITY 49

Pose like a superhero and say with conviction (like you mean it):

"I HAVE THE POWER TO TAKE CONTROL OF MY FEELINGS, THINKING, AND ACTIONS!"

ACTIVITY 50

Identify a trigger that is difficult for you to deal with. Answer the following **Stop, Think, and Go** questions to come up with a plan for how you can deal with the trigger when faced with it.

STOP: What is the trigger? What are your thoughts about it? How do you feel about it?

THINK: What are three different choices that you can make when faced with this trigger?

GO: What would each choice cause? How would that make you feel? Pick the choice that would be best for you.

A PARENT'S GUIDE TO
Self-Regulation
A Practical Framework for Breaking the Cycle of Dysregulation and Mastering Emotions for Parents and Children
Dr. Amber Thornton
Clinical Psychologist

THE
SELF-REGULATION
HANDBOOK FOR TEENS & YOUNG ADULTS
A Trauma-Informed Guide to Fostering Personal Resilience and Enhancing Interpersonal Skills
Kathy P. Wu, PhD

ABOUT THE AUTHOR

Jenna Berman is a therapist in Montclair, New Jersey. She received a degree in psychology from Hobart and William Smith Colleges, a master's degree in social work from Columbia University, and post-graduate training at the Ackerman Institute for the Family and NYU. Jenna has a range of experience working in outpatient mental health, school, residential, and medical settings. Jenna is passionate about helping children and adolescents feel empowered to overcome obstacles and reach their potential. She currently resides in Montclair, New Jersey, with her husband Colin, their children Natasha and Teddy, and their two cats Benson and Stabler.